The "Building A High Performance Team" guide presents valuable information and ideas on key topics including onboarding, rewarding, and recognizing employees.

The expectations and responsibilities of managers and employees are described to enhance productive working relationships.

I0394753

This guide was compiled by
"Total Impact Employee Solutions (T.I.E.S)",
a consulting group operating with an
experienced management team of
Human Resource and Benefit professionals.

The company specializes in employee engagement, morale, wellness, and retention planning. Additional services and products are available and can be customized to address the needs and priorities of your business.

Web Site: http://www.totalimpactsol.com
Phone: 1-800-717-0978
Fax: 1-888-211-9482

© 2013, Total Impact Employee Solutions
#0513

CONTENTS

Building a High Performance Team   *4*

Onboarding   *5*

Managing the Team   *8*

Feedback   *14*

Recognize and Reward   *16*

Surprise Your Employees   *19*

Employees' Responsibilities   *21*

The Ribbon Ceremony   *23*

Open Forum   *24*

Acknowledgements   *25*

About the Authors   *26*

A GUIDE TO BUILDING A HIGH PERFORMANCE TEAM

*To accomplish great things,
we must dream as well as act!*

BUILDING A HIGH PERFORMANCE TEAM is no easy task. It takes vision, a team to buy into the vision, and the dedication to do the hard work to ensure success.

Ideally, a high performance team should understand how to work hard and play hard because enjoyment of the job and the work environment is essential to the success of any team.

Loyalty is priceless.

➤ Onboarding

Prior to start date

* Communicate with the new employee regarding where to report, the time, and the person with whom to meet, and any documents that may be required on the first day of employment.

* Communicate to the team regarding the addition of a new employee - name, title, position, start date, and background or experience.

* Answer questions regarding the new team member's responsibilities and role on the team.

* Ensure a workspace is set up complete with desk, computer, printer, phone, supplies, manuals, company directory, and business cards (if applicable).

* Establish access to software applications, email systems, shared calendars, and other technical tools needed for the position.

Start date

* Welcome the new employee with a small banner, card, and/or flowers at his/her work station.

* Introduce to department members. Include a brief description of each team member's primary area of responsibilities.

* Provide a phone list of team members, partners, vendors, and various business locations and contacts.

* Tour work areas, departments, break rooms, restrooms, and reception areas.

* Review general information: work start/end times, lunch or break periods, department meeting schedules, and parking.

* Discuss job description and expectations.

* Discuss employee benefits and policies and procedures. Identify resources such as a handbook, online information, manager, or an HR representative.

* Review company structure, executives and senior officers (names, titles, and area of responsibility).

* Assign a department "buddy" to assist with routine questions.

* Provide a summary of emergency procedures and contact information. Be sure to obtain the new employee's contact data and record it appropriately.

* If you are a proponent of an open-door policy, make sure you are truly available for your employees when they need you.

* Review your "open-door policy" and reinforce it regularly. Encourage the employee to set an appointment time with you to discuss questions or concerns.

Within 1 week

* Prepare a Welcome New Employee announcement and distribute to all departments (include employee's duties/phone/email, etc.).

* Introduce the employee to key executives (as available).

* Introduce employee to other support department members.

* Schedule a "manager–employee" meeting to address questions, assess the onboarding experience, and discuss next steps (for example: training).

➢ Managing the Team

* **Policies, procedures, and processes.** Everyone knows the importance of having and following prescribed procedures that are in place. These are the life blood of any department and should be improved upon as the department and its employees evolve.

   Every individual should have a copy of the policies, procedures, processes, and should be held accountable for following them.

* **Organizing/prioritizing/time management.** Some employees struggle more than others with managing their time. Identify the person who seems to be good at this and have them coach those who need assistance. Provide follow-up sessions to assess progress.

* **Work/life balance.** Allow your staff to have a balanced life. Work is important but employees deserve to have quality time with their families. They are more apt to work extra hours if they feel they are not being robbed of time with their families on a regular basis.

* **Be a motivator**. Recognize when their attitude, work ethic, or passion change. Address the issue immediately.

* **Buddy system.** You can have great fun with this! The system can be instrumental in developing team spirit. Buddies look out for one another; they should know when a team member is stressed or overwhelmed and provide the necessary encouragement or assistance.

    Buddies ensure that the work is flowing and deadlines are being met. Having a buddy system that works right is like having a best friend. The camaraderie brings an enjoyment to the office environment that makes coming to work so much more satisfying.

* **Skill assessments.** Know your team! They may have a particular job title and skill set but, chances are, they have capabilities in other areas. Find out what those skills are and use them! You will see a positive difference in engagement and productivity. You will be able to identify employees who can be involved with special projects and assignments. It's a great opportunity for employees to demonstrate their special skills. Sit back and watch them shine!

    Assessment tools can uncover areas where skill development is needed or additional training is warranted. This will help employees focus on improving their deficiencies before they become a performance issue.

* **Subject Matter Experts (SMEs).** Identify areas where team members can excel and assign them to the SME role (for example: research, problem solving, technical skills, etc.).

* **Set a standard for excellence.** A high-performing team cannot be associated with mediocrity. Never settle for being average. The team should have a reputation for excellence in everything it does.

* **Teach boundaries and interpersonal skills.** This will enhance the abilities of your employees to effectively work with other team members, partners, and clients.

* **Emphasize that rewards are based on performance and results.** A good relationship with your staff is paramount but it is essential your employees do not expect to be rewarded for poor performance.

* **Command respect on their behalf.** Do not allow other managers or employees to demean your staff. Be a staunch supporter for your team. Apply discipline with kindness, understanding, patience, and in private.

* **Be their cheerleader.** Let them get to know and trust you. Keep their confidence unless it is something that directly impacts the department. If you have to break their confidence, explain why.

* **Be kind, be fair, and be a coach.** People tend to underestimate the power of kindness. Many seem to think it has no place in the work place but there is nothing to be gained from ruling by intimidation or emotion. It simply breeds resentment and resentment breeds disloyalty.

* **Show your employees you value them.** Acknowledge employees with a greeting, a question about their work or family, and always use common courtesies.

* **Let them know how hard it would be to get the job done without them.** Do you genuinely feel they are an asset? If you do, let them know it.

    If you don't, figure out why and fix it. Is additional training necessary? Is there something personal that's holding them back or are they bored and disenchanted with the job? Are you focusing on their strengths? Ask them!

* **Be interested in their families and community involvement.** Do you know what makes your employees tick? Do you know about special occasions in their lives? Show interest and notice their reaction.

* **Involve your entire team in department meetings, training, celebrations, and other events.** Don't make the mistake of leaving off-site team members in the dark. They are a part of the team and should not feel they are insignificant because they are not at the main location.

* **In order for the department to function to its full capacity, every team member should have the same opportunity to receive training, recognition, and important information timely.**

   It will take an extra effort to make yourself available and coordinate schedules to accomplish this, but it must be done.

* **Teachable moments.** During your department meetings, have team members share an event that occurred, negative or positive. Have the employee describe the situation, the actions taken, and the outcome. There should be a lesson learned from every experience.

* **Share excerpts from good books, news articles or industry reports.** Have lively discussions and see how the information can be used to advance the team.

* **Open Forum.** These meetings allow employees to address concerns or disputes in a safe, non-threatening, and confidential arena. *(See page 24 for the rules to effectively conduct an open forum).*

* **Inclusion and respect for everyone should be the philosophy of your department.** Talk about it, demonstrate it, and expect it.

* **Encourage employees to stand up for themselves and others within company protocol.** The strong and confident can guide and support those who are not.

* **Support fair salaries and provide the tools that allow employees to be effective in their jobs.** Few employees are equipped to fight the battle over salaries and tools. A good manager ensures the team has both.

* **Do not be afraid to assess your own behavior.** It is important that your demeanor is one of approachability and invites interaction with your team. Make changes to your management style as appropriate.

"The time is always right to Do what is right".

--- Martin Luther King, Jr.

➢ **Feedback**

* **One-on-one discussions**. These are invaluable in building good relationships. They are times of open and honest conversation. The employee should be encouraged and allowed to speak freely and confidentially without concern for repercussion.

  This is also a great time to mentor, recognize, and empower the employee to excel.

  You should also use this time to solicit feedback on your personal performance. You will be surprised at their insight and how this information will help you grow as a leader.

* **Group huddles.** These are quick informal meetings that allow you to address issues or pass on vital information if there is no time for a department meeting.

* **Written performance reviews.** In addition to addressing areas of current weakness, talk about improvements that have been made throughout the year. Identify strengths. State your pride in their areas of achievement.

  Provide specific examples of performance in formal reviews. This will reinforce the fact that you recognize what they are doing and how well they are performing. A review, when done thoroughly and respectfully, can spur an employee to greater improvement and achievement.

* **Discuss skills and strengths.** This is an important topic in building employee engagement. When you identify their capabilities, employees will look for opportunities to use their strengths and shine. Employees become aware of their potential and are better able to shift their focus on specific areas to improve skills. These types of discussions can be the foundation for employees to identify additional career paths.

* **Provide discipline and coaching when necessary.** Always conduct in private and balance with recognition.

* **Support and hold employees accountable.** They should know it is okay to make a mistake as long as they own it and correct it. Coach employees on this concept.

➢ Recognize and Reward

Catch your employees doing something good. Recognize it and reward them with a Rah Rah moment or note.

* Rah Rah moments. This is one of our favorite ways to recognize employees. Get everyone's attention and recognize them publicly in the presence of their colleagues. Notice the light in their eyes and the pride and joy in their smiles

* For those who aren't receiving a Rah Rah at that particular time, encourage them to cheer for their colleague, knowing that their time will certainly come.

* Rah Rah notes. As an alternative to the Rah Rah moment, place a Rah Rah note on the employee's desk or in his/her work area.

* Advise upper management of an employee's unique skills and talents.

* Give the employee the opportunity to work on special projects. This will not only empower the employee but will give him/her a boost in confidence.

* Publicize their achievements. You can do this in the company's newsletter, at company meetings, or at manager or department meetings.

* Have formal celebrations. Invite other department leaders and recognize employees with certificates, plaques, etc. These rewards do not have to be expensive. The mere fact that management took time out of their busy day to be a part of the recognition will delight them.

* Start something new in your department and possibly throughout your organization. Give ribbons of recognition and appreciation. Provide the employee with an extra ribbon to pass on to someone else who is deserving. (*See page 24 for the idea behind the ribbon and its use*).

* Create positions or revise duties where possible to give employees a career path. Give those who have earned it the opportunity to show their leadership skills; for example, team leaders with limited supervisory authority who can assist you in managing the department. This will reinforce their value and allow them to show their capabilities.

* Use a coveted parking space as a reward for employees who have done something outstanding.

* If policy permits, designate a casual day for long work days or successful completion of a project.

* Have a work area redecorating party or contest.

* Arrange for lunch with an executive.

➢ Surprise Your Employees
FIND WAYS TO KEEP THEM SMILING!

* Do activities together that are not work related. Encourage them to work hard and play hard. Be creative and use what is available. Here are some examples that proved successful:

    Picnic on the floor – keep it simple! Have the team bring in items for a picnic. Find an open spot on the floor, spread out the blanket and have a picnic lunch together. Make it fun!

    Big hat (or favorite hat) luncheon – everyone brings in a dish and clothes for a dress-up lunch. You can have this in a safe, enclosed area of the parking lot, on the lawn, or anywhere that the company would allow. The team changes clothes and goes to the event. Have someone take pictures and share them.

    You are in for an unbelievable event and when you return to work, the productivity is unmatched.

* Let them WOW you. Encourage contests to gather ideas. Implement as many ideas as are feasible and valuable to the department and/or the company.

* Inspirational thoughts or quotes. Ask team members to provide the group with one each week. Encourage them to embrace it and live it!

* Thank their families for supporting them during busy times, long hours and giving-up family time for the company. Send thank you cards, movie tickets, dinner tickets, or invite them to a picnic in the park.

Some of the things you do to keep morale high will seem elementary but if they work for your team, GO FOR IT!!!

These activities proved successful in developing our high performance team. Don't be afraid to think outside the box and encourage employee suggestions. YOU may be surprised!

A gifted leader is capable of touching your heart.

EMPLOYEES' RESPONSIBILITY

BE...

* <u>Professional</u> - be professional in your speech, your conduct, and how you present yourself.

    Remember, someone is always watching and you never get a second chance to make a first impression. Image matters!

* <u>Enthusiastic</u> – do you love what you're doing? Even if you don't, you applied for and accepted the position. Give it your best and, if you can't, move on.

    Your employer deserves your best, your customers deserve your best, your team deserves your best, and you deserve your best!

* Honest – are you giving 100% or are you just getting by? Do you spend your time figuring out how to make things better or are you too busy watching the clock? Don't steal your employer's time or waste your own!

* Coachable - a manager has the responsibility to develop and provide a positive work environment.

  An employee's responsibility is to demonstrate a willingness to learn new things, be open to constructive criticism, and have the desire to do what it takes to ensure the success of the department.

* Engaged - are you involved in the daily activities of the department? Do you offer new ideas?

  Do you care about the quality of your work? Do you excel in customer relations? Are you a team player?

  BE THE EXAMPLE FOR YOUR TEAM!

"The first great gift we bestow on others is a good example". --- Thomas Morell

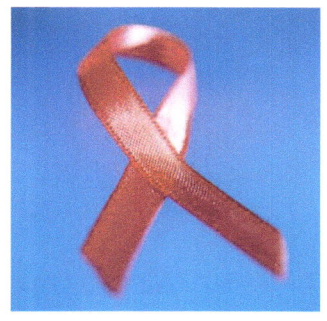

THE RIBBON CEREMONY

A simple acknowledgment, be it a kind word, a smile, or a RIBBON OF ENCOURAGEMENT, can change someone's day, attitude or life.

Use a ribbon as a symbol of recognition. Have a ceremony and pin your deserving employees with a ribbon which displays terms such as, **Pride** (I am proud of your accomplishments), **Gratitude** (I am grateful for all that you do), and **Honor** (I honor you for the person you are).

Give the recipient(s) an additional ribbon and ask them to pass it on to someone who is worthy of the recognition.

Start a movement throughout your department and the company that will positively impact morale.

This idea was inspired by the e-Rumor: The Blue Ribbon that Saved a Teen's Life.

"It is better to deserve honors and not have them than to have them and not deserve them". -- Aristotle

OPEN FORUM: RULES OF ENGAGEMENT

1. Privately approach the team member with whom there is a disagreement. Request a time and place to discuss a resolution that accommodates both parties. (Meeting should take place within a day or two of conflict.)
2. Remain calm and keep a professional demeanor. Be open and honest.
3. Do not discuss the conflict with another team member or employee who is not involved.
4. Avoid name calling, placing blame, and comments such as: "You always" or "You never".
5. Listen intently to the other person's viewpoint. Allow them time to talk without interruption.
6. Each individual involved should provide solutions and explore each possibility.
7. Role play, if necessary, to see the full picture.
8. Select the best solution and commit to the plan of action.
9. If both team members are unable to reach an agreement, the dispute should be discussed with an objective individual being the mediator.
10. If there is no resolution, the matter should be escalated to a manager and/or Human Resource representative.
11. Once dispute has been resolved, it should not be rehashed.

Acknowledgements:

This guide is dedicated to the B.E.S.T. (BENEFITS ENROLLMENT SERVICE TEAM), one of the most dedicated, loyal, productive, and fun loving teams ever assembled. Individually and collectively, they were simply STELLAR!

To our valued colleagues, focus group participants, and community business leaders - thank you for sharing your time, energy, knowledge, and expertise.

Special thanks to our families and friends for their support and encouragement.

Your contributions, suggestions and guidance are greatly appreciated!

Authors of "Building A High Performance Team" Guide

Cledline Taylor has always had a passion for people. Having completed Liberal Arts courses at the University of the West Indies she worked with and gained inspiration from young adults for twelve years. A career change saw her becoming a manager after three years in the hospitality industry. Then followed sixteen years in the banking industry where, as a Human Resource professional, she was not only a benefits supervisor but also a payroll specialist, employee relations specialist, and recruiting specialist. Cledline has 28 years of HR experience in several industries. In her most recent role, she was a Benefits Training Specialist, Supervisor and Manager for over 11 years. Cledline successfully completed numerous courses in supervision, management, and customer service. She received certifications through the Florida Banking Institute, Dale Carnegie School, and most recently completed a program on Leadership Skills for Success. She is a 2-15 licensed Florida Insurance Agent.

Carla Randle is a Human Resource professional who has worked in the HR field for over 19 years, both in the profit and non-profit sectors. Carla's primary responsibilities included benefits administration, recruitment, and customer relations training. Her career includes HR Benefits Specialist, Customer Service Coordinator, and Financial Coordinator. She is a graduate of Palm Beach Atlantic University and earned a B.S. in Organizational Management, majoring in Human Resource Management. She is a 2-15 licensed Florida Insurance Agent and a Notary Public.

Karen Good has over 30 years of experience in education, government, and with both small and large corporations. During her 20 years in HR, Karen's responsibilities included sales and technical training, employee development, resolution of complex employee relations issues, recruiting, hiring, and displacements. She was also responsible for HR compliance, compensation administration, metrics, reporting and budgeting. Karen implemented and trained all levels of employees on performance management programs and HR self-service tools. Karen advised and consulted with executive and senior management, was a member of Senior Leadership committees and special task force groups. Her HR positions included Training Director, AVP Employment Manager, VP Human Resource Director, and VP Senior HR Business Partner. From 1993-2012 she held her certification as a Professional in Human Resources (PHR). Karen received her B.S. and M.A. in Human Resources and Education from West Virginia University.